English Olympiad

Book 3

www.pegasusforkids.com

© **B. Jain Publishers (P) Ltd.** All rights reserved. No part of this book may be reproduced, stored in a retrieval system or transmitted, in any form or by any means, mechanical, photocopying, recording or otherwise, without any prior written permission of the publisher.

Published by Kuldeep Jain for B. Jain Publishers (P) Ltd., D-157, Sector 63, Noida - 201307, U.P.

Registered office: 1921/10, Chuna Mandi, Paharganj, New Delhi-110055

Printed in India at Narain Printers & Binder, Noida

Preface

English Olympiad Book–3 has been carefully written, designed and brought to fruition keeping in mind the requirements of the students. It has almost all necessary elements that make each exercise a learning experience for the children, their teachers and parents.

'Learning by doing' – the ethos behind introducing Olympiads is an effort to achieve perfection. In this spirit, we have followed a systematic pattern, inclusive of the scientific method and child-centric approach, wherein each concept has been explained again (as understood that it was done as part of grammar lessons). Therefore, revisions here leave enough room to substantiate upon experiential learning that help students to deliver better.

In the end of the book, we have also provided three test papers that carry a diverse set of questions. It will help children test themselves amidst all concepts put together in random order, which will bring greater degree of clarity and thought.

Salient Features

- Multiple choice questions
- Use of necessary illustrations to make learning simpler
- Model test papers in the end to make a wholesome assessment
- Inclusion of almost all aspects of English Olympiad exams

We wish all readers of **English Olympiad Book–3** a joyful experience.

Contents

1. Comprehension 5
2. Types of Sentences 14
3. Subject and Predicate 17
4. Nouns 20
5. More Kinds of Nouns 23
6. Pronouns 28
7. Verbs 31
8. Prepositions 35
9. Conjunctions 38
10. Articles 41
11. Jumbled Words 44
12. Jumbled Words in Sentences 47
13. Antonyms and Synonyms 49
14. Story Writing 52
15. Analogy 54
    Model Test Paper-1 56
    Model Test Paper-2 60
    Model Test Paper-3 64

Answer Key 68

Comprehension

Comprehension is the ability to read a text and understand its meaning. It lets you:

- Develop vocabulary knowledge.

- Understand a given text as a whole.

- Answer the questions related to the topic and draw conclusions.

Passage 1

Read the passage given below and answer the questions correctly.

Dolphins are very intelligent and they are loved by humans. They have been able to fascinate us in a variety of ways. They are curious, form strong bonds within their pod, and they have been known to help humans in a variety of ways including rescues and entertainment.

There are 43 different species of dolphins that have been recognised, out of which 38 are marine dolphins which are those that we are the most aware of and five of them are river dolphins. It can be very interesting to look at each of these species separately instead of dolphins as a whole.

They are very entertaining due to the leaps that they make out of the water. Some of them leap up to 30 feet in the air. They have to come to the surface of the water at different intervals to get air. This interval to get air can be anything from 20 seconds to 30 minutes. The body of the dolphin is greyish blue and the skin is very sensitive to human touch and to other things that could be in the water.

Even though dolphins are wonderful creatures that seem to be extremely intelligent and friendly, we still are a huge threat for dolphins. We must respect these great animals that everybody likes, but most know so little about.

EXERCISE 1

Choose the correct options.

1. **Dolphin is a very intelligent:**
   a) bird   b) insect
   c) reptile   d) mammal

2. **Dolphins form strong bonds within their:**
   a) flock   b) herd
   c) swarm   d) pod

3. **How many different species of dolphins have been recognised?**
   a) 50   b) 24
   c) 48   d) 43

4. **Why do dolphins come to the surface of the water?**
   a) to breathe   b) to eat
   c) to play   d) to dance

5. **Who is a huge threat to dolphins?**
   a) crocodiles   b) humans
   c) ships   d) frogs

EXERCISE 2

Choose the correct antonyms.

1. **Intelligent**
   a) Smart
   b) Foolish
   c) Small
   d) Long

2. **Loved**
   a) Admired
   b) Big
   c) Low
   d) Hated

3. **Strong**
   a) Pretty
   b) Far
   c) Weak
   d) Near

4. **Agree**
   a) Find
   b) Hope
   c) Disagree
   d) Like

5. **Respect**
   a) Huge
   b) Inside
   c) Angry
   d) Disrespect

Passage 2

Read the passage given below and answer the questions correctly.

New Delhi is the capital of India. It is a beautiful city. It stands on the banks of river Yamuna. Delhi is a very old city and has even been mentioned in Mahabharata as Indraprastha. After that also, Delhi has seen many other rulers like the Aryans, Mughals and Britishers.

Delhi is divided into two parts — Old Delhi and New Delhi. New Delhi is very beautiful. The Old Delhi was constructed during the Mughal period. In New Delhi, there are beautiful parks and gardens. Nehru Park, Talkatora Garden, Lodhi Garden and Buddha Park are worth seeing.

Old Delhi has several symbols of great historical importance like the Red Fort, Jama Masjid and Chandni Chowk. Delhi's old buildings remind us about its glorious past. People come to Delhi to see historical places like Qutab Minar, Parliament House, National Museum, Gurudwara Sis Ganj and India Gate.

Delhi is a great centre of trade, industry and education. Karol Bagh, Connaught Place and Lajpat Nagar are famous markets of the city.

EXERCISE 3

Choose the correct options.

1. **What is the capital of India?**
   a) Mumbaib) Chennai
   c) New Delhid) Kolkata

2. **On which river banks is Delhi situated?**
   a) Gangab) Narmada
   c) Kosid) Yamuna

3. **During which period was Old Delhi constructed?**
   a) Britishb) Aryan
   c) Mughald) Maurya

4. **By what name is Delhi mentioned in Mahabharata?**

   a) Pataliputra   b) Hastinapur

   c) Kannauj   d) Indraprastha

5. **Delhi has many symbols of _____ importance.**

   a) musical   b) agricultural

   c) scientific   d) historical

EXERCISE 4

Make sentences with the following words.

1. River   _____

2. Trade   _____

3. Beautiful _____

4. City   _____

5. Great   _____

Passage 3

Read the passage given below and answer the questions correctly.

The wheel is perhaps man's greatest invention. The cart, the bicycle, the motor car and the railway train, all move on wheels. Even an aircraft which flies thousands of kilometres through the air needs wheels for taking-off and landing. It is not only important for transport but also for machines that produce various goods for us, watches that tell us the time, generators that produce electricity and many gadgets which have become a part our day-to-day life. They cannot work without some form of wheel.

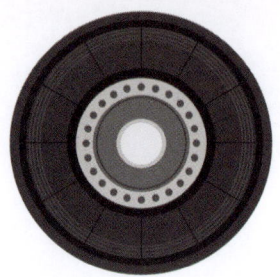   

Before the invention of the wheel, it was very difficult to travel long distances. Travellers carried their belongings on their backs and faced many dangers on the way. Very few, therefore, dared to travel. Even those who undertook a journey did not know when they would reach their destination and whether they would return home safely. Wheel was invented around 5000 years ago, it is not correct. According to western history wheel was invented in Mospotamiya (Iraq) in B.C. 3500. According to our mythology wheel was present in Ramayana in B.C. 5000. It means wheel was present before 7500 years from today. So, pls chk this fact again.

But as a matter of fact, no one knows who the inventor of wheel was. Thousands and thousands of years ago an unknown person invented this simple device which has become one of the most important tools for man today.

EXERCISE 5

Choose the correct options.

1. **What is man's greatest invention?**
   a) car   b) aircraft
   c) wheel   d) train

2. **Before the invention of wheel, it was very difficult to:**
   a) cook food   b) sleep
   c) swim   d) travel long distances

3. **For what else other than transport is wheel important?**
   a) animals   b) plants
   c) birds   d) other machines

4. **How did people carry heavy loads before the invention of wheel?**

   a) in their hands
   b) on boats
   c) on their backs
   d) didn't carry at all

EXERCISE 6

Choose the correct synonyms for the following words.

1. **Invention**
   a) Creation
   b) Emotion
   c) Notion
   d) Ration

2. **Travel**
   a) Journey
   b) Fight
   c) Speed
   d) Light

3. **produce**
   a) Break
   b) Make
   c) Freeze
   d) Dive

4. **Danger**
   a) Rough
   b) Life
   c) Smooth
   d) Risk

5. **Goods**
   a) Steps
   b) Door
   c) Finish
   d) Products

Passage 4

Read the passage given below and answer the questions correctly.

A mouse was having a very bad time. She could find no food at all. She looked here and there, but there was no food, and she grew very thin.

At last the mouse found a basket full of corn. There was a small hole in the basket, and she crept in. She could just get through the hole.

Then she began to eat the corn. As she was very hungry, she ate a great deal, and went on eating and eating. She had grown very fat before she felt that she had had enough.

When the mouse tried to climb out of the basket, she could not. She was too fat to pass through the hole.

"How shall I climb out?" said the mouse, "Oh, how shall I climb out?"

Just then a squirrel was passing by, and he heard the mouse.

"Mouse," said the squirrel, "if you want to climb out of the basket, you must wait till you have grown as thin as you were when you went in."

EXERCISE 7

Choose the correct options.

1. **The mouse was having a bad time because:**
   a) she was tired
   b) she was angry
   c) she was upset
   d) she was hungry

2. **What did the mouse find?**
   a) a pot
   b) a cup
   c) a basket
   d) a sack

3. **What was in the basket?**
   a) peanuts
   b) cake
   c) corn
   d) fruits

4. How did the mouse become after eating the corn?

   a) very tall   b) very small

   c) very heavy   d) very fat

5. Who was passing by the basket?

   a) squirrel   b) hen

   c) dog   d) rabbit

EXERCISE 8

Choose the correct words from the brackets and fill in the blanks.

1. **There was no _____, and she grew very thin.**

   a) food   b) water

   c) thin   d) old

2. **At last the mouse found a _____, full of corn.**

   a) car   b) basket

   c) corn   d) wheat

3. **Just then a _____ was passing by and he heard the mouse.**

   a) dog   b) squirrel

   c) mouse   d) rat

4. **As she was very _____, she ate a lot, and went on eating and eating.**

   a) tired   b) hungry

   c) drinking   d) eating

TYPES OF SENTENCES

Bird: What is name?

Squirrel: What are you asking?

Bird: I name Neo, What are you?

Squirrel: I am still not able to understand what you are saying.

The squirrel was not able to understand what Neo was saying because Neo's words were not making any sense.

What is a sentence?

A sentence is a group of words that makes complete sense. It starts with a capital letter and ends with a full stop, an exclamation mark or a question mark.

We use sentences to talk to each other. Written sentences let us understand what the writer wants to convey. A sentence expresses a complete thought.

There are four types of sentences.

1. **Declarative sentence:** A sentence that is a statement and tells something.
2. **Imperative sentence:** A sentence that gives direction or a command.
3. **Exclamatory sentence:** A sentence that shows strong feeling.
4. **Interrogative sentence:** A sentence that asks a question.

EXERCISE 1

Which of the following are sentences? Write YES or NO.

1. Corns grow in the fields. _____

2. Over the grass. _____

3. The driver of the car. _____

4. Let us fly a kite today. _____

5. In the basket. _____

6. Switch off the lights, please. _____

7. Waiting for dinner. _____

8. Close the bag. _____

9. Where is the salt? _____

10. On the tree. _____

EXERCISE 2

Make one sentence of each type given below using the word holiday.

1. **Interrogative** _____
2. **Declarative** _____
3. **Imperative** _____
4. **Exclamatory** _____

EXERCISE 3

Rewrite the following paragraph with capital letters and full stops wherever required.

peter and nancy are brother and sister peter is nine and nancy is eleven years old they live in the city near a school they play after school they also help their mother in the evening

EXERCISE 4

Tick (✓) D for declarative, I for interrogative, E for exclamatory and IM for imperative sentences:

1. **What should I buy for Saurabh on his birthday?**
   D   I ✓   E   IM

2. **I only have hundred rupees to spend.**
   D ✓   I   E   IM

3. **Oh! I lost my book!**
   D   I   E ✓   IM

4. **Call him immediately.**
   D   I   E   IM ✓

5. **We are going to the Shoe House!**
   D   I   E ✓   IM

6. **Do you know where he lives?**
   D   I ✓   E   IM

7. **I have been attending guitar classes for two days.**
   D ✓   I   E   IM

8. **Do not swim in deep water.**
   D   I   E   IM ✓

9. **Has Ashu plucked the flowers?**
   D   I ✓   E   IM

10. **The children play on the seesaw in the park.**
    D ✓   I   E   IM

Subject and Predicate

3

The subject of a sentence tells us who or what the sentence is about. The predicate of a sentence tells what the subject does, did, is or was. The predicate contains a verb that tells action or a state of being.

For example:

The man is singing in the park.

Subject - The man   **Predicate** - is singing in the park.

EXERCISE 1

Write a suitable subject and complete the following sentences.

1. _____ has closed the gate of the school.

2. _____ grow in the forest.

3. _____ is big and scary.

4. _____ hung itself on the wall.

5. _____ is falling down the stream.

6. _____ flew back to its hive.

7. _____ sleeps in the old armchair.

8. _____ stopped to pick us from the airport.

9. _____ lives on a farm in Assam.

10. At the football game, _____ won by one goal.

EXERCISE 2

Write a predicate to complete each sentence given below.

1. Only a few people _____

2. Elephants _____

3. Fresh vegetables _____

4. The old man _____

5. The other side of the market _____

6. The pretty woman_____

7. Saurabh, the carpenter_____

8. The little child_____

9. The famous actor_____

10. The new school building_____

EXERCISE 3

Find the subject in each sentence given below.

1. **The horse ran in the field.**

    a) horse   b) horse ran

    c) ran in   d) he field

2. **The people in the house are having a party.**

    a) in the house   b) having a party

    c) people   d) house are having

3. **Mom asked me to go to the store.**

   a) Mom b) asked me to go

   c) to go to d) the store

4. **The president spoke to the people.**

   a) president spoke b) spoke to

   c) the people d) president

5. **Jenny rode her bicycle to school.**

   a) Jenny b) bike

   c) rode d) to school

Nouns

Look at the words given in colour:

There is a **notebook** for you.

Rohan is riding a beautiful **bicycle**.

Oh! There is a **cat** in the corner.

We are moving to **London** next year.

The words: **notebook**, **Rohan**, **bicycle**, **cat** and **London**, name a person, things and places around us. **Noun is a word that names a person, place, animal or thing.** They are also known as **naming words**.

Kinds of Nouns

Proper Noun – name of a particular person, place or thing like, Delhi, Robin or Hollywood, etc.

Common Noun – name of any person, place, animal or thing like, fan, table, book, car, etc.

EXERCISE 1

Write any four nouns for each heading.

1. Person _____, _____, _____, _____,

2. Place _____, _____, _____, _____,

3. Animal _____, _____, _____, _____,

4. Thing _____, _____, _____, _____,

EXERCISE 2

Identify proper noun or common noun.

Red Fort	Mickey Mouse	Sunday
dog	Mars	game
man	Christmas	Rima
city	month	country

EXERCISE 3

Circle the nouns in the words given below.

1. woman   sweet   flower

   kind   book

2. school   run   city

   black   cat

3. went   chips   five

   crying   beautiful

4. England   house   long

   boy   with

5. music   gone   spent

   blue   fire

Underline the proper nouns in the words given below.

1.	India	Game	Evening	Road
2.	October	Shop	Gift	Birthday
3.	Audi	Doctor	Elephant	Film
4.	Cat	Aunt	Bible	Boys
5.	Book	Sydney	Highway	Action
6.	Diwali	Special	Festival	Celebration
7.	Amazon	Chocolate	Muffin	Toy
8.	Asia	Continent	Land	Rivers
9.	Earth	Single	Life	Planet
10.	Sam	Man	Young	Gentle
11.	Professor	Mouse	Christmas	Laptop
12.	Batman	Smart	Good	Fighter
13.	New Delhi	City	Market	Angel
14.	Storybook	Wall	Google	Computer
15.	Student	Class	Girl	Naina

More Kinds of Nouns

5

There are three more kinds of **nouns** other than **proper** and **common nouns**.

1. **Collective Noun** – name of a collection or group of things, animals or people like, team, army, herd or bunch.

2. **Material Noun** – name of a substance like milk, cloth, iron or wood.

3. **Abstract Noun** – name of quality, state, feeling or idea like, happy, honesty, pain, advice.

EXERCISE 1

Fill in the blanks with correct collective nouns.

1. **I have lost a _____ of keys.**
    a) bunch   b) group
    c) set   d) collection

2. **There seems to be a plan behind this _____ of events.**
    a) bundle   b) chain
    c) series   d) group

3. **There is a large _____ of fish near the coast.**
    a) shoal   b) troupe
    c) gang   d) army

23

4. Do not disturb that _____ of bees.
   a) swarm   b) herd
   c) cattle   d) flock

5. There is a fine _____ of paintings in the palace.
   a) group   b) collection
   c) bundle   d) stack

6. The _____ of players can reach anytime now.
   a) choir   b) army
   c) team   d) troupe

7. The police could not control the _____.
   a) crowd   b) herd
   c) cattle   d) swarm

8. The _____ of birds flew away instantly.
   a) flock   b) company
   c) colony   d) cluster

9. I would be gifting them a _____ of flowers.
   a) bunch   b) bouquet
   c) set   d) army

10. The _____ of mountains is far from here.
    a) school   b) range
    c) colony   d) pack

EXERCISE 2

Circle the abstract nouns in the following.

happiness	Ganges	sadness	kindness	king
strength	bravery	excitement	children	hope
soldiers	army	Mohit	confidence	sorrow

EXERCISE 3

Choose the correct abstract noun and fill in the blanks.

1. **You should not get _____ because of such things.**
   a) tense
   b) laugh
   c) small
   d) over

2. **An elephant has great _____.**
   a) weakness
   b) smile
   c) speed
   d) strength

3. **Great men are known for their _____.**
   a) foolishness
   b) height
   c) anger
   d) wisdom

4. **We do not need your _____.**
   a) help
   b) stop
   c) fight
   d) pull

5. **The story shows Alice's _____.**
   a) smartness
   b) anger
   c) laziness
   d) intelligence

6. **Children are loved for their _____ .**
   a) innocence
   b) health
   c) moods
   d) sorrow

7. **It was such a _____ when our team lost the match.**
   a) disappointment
   b) enjoyment
   c) fun
   d) grief

8. **Rajeev gave the speech with _____ .**
   a) anger
   b) strength
   c) laugh
   d) confidence

9. **The old woman was so _____ that she cut the goose open.**
   a) funny
   b) greedy
   c) smart
   d) upset

10. **Neena made a poster on _____ .**
    a) friendship
    b) permission
    c) reason
    d) tired

EXERCISE 4

Fill in the blanks with correct material nouns.

1. **Fresh _____ is always good for health.**
   a) food
   b) nuts
   c) ice cream
   d) box

2. **The jewellery made of _____ is very expensive.**
   a) gold
   b) stone
   c) paper
   d) glass

3. **No matter how much you try, you cannot move that _____.**
   a) rock
   b) pen
   c) feather
   d) box

4. **A car runs on _____.**
   a) honey
   b) water
   c) petrol
   d) cheese

5. **You are not well so please take some _____.**
   a) medicine
   b) burger
   c) cake
   d) chips

6. **The _____ is coming off the walls.**
   a) fan
   b) paint
   c) bulb
   d) door

7. **Vegetable _____ is used for cooking food.**
   a) oil
   b) water
   c) paste
   d) salad

8. **This _____ smells very nice.**
   a) dish
   b) tap
   c) brick
   d) marble

9. **People still use _____ for cooking food.**
   a) cement
   b) wood
   c) petrol
   d) stones

10. **This pole is made of _____.**
    a) iron
    b) paper
    c) water
    d) mud

PRONOUNS

Sam tells his mother about his best friend Anna.

My best friend is **Anna**. **Anna** is a good girl. **Anna** comes first in class. **Anna's** teachers love **Anna**.

Which word is repeated by Sam five times in the above lines?

It is the name of his friend Anna.

He can also say:

My best friend is **Anna**. **She** is a good girl. **She** comes first in class. **Her** teachers love **her**.

The words **she** and **her** are used in place of Anna. They are called **pronouns**.

A **pronoun** is a word that can be used in place of a noun.

EXERCISE 1

Which of the given words in the following sentences is pronoun?

1. **She went to the store with Megha.**
   a) She
   b) went
   c) store
   d) the

2. **Six of us had to fit in the tiny car.**
   a) fit
   b) tiny
   c) us
   d) Six

3. **Every Thursday, Mayank goes to the market with them.**
   a) Every
   b) goes
   c) market
   d) them

4. **At the store, the cashier gave her some change.**
   a) cashier
   b) change
   c) her
   d) At

5. **When the Sun comes up, he leaves for work.**
   a) when
   b) Sun
   c) work
   d) he

6. **I enjoyed seeing them on the playground.**
   a) enjoyed
   b) I and them
   c) playground
   d) the

7. **Have you hung the painting on the wall yet?**
   a) you
   b) painting
   c) wall
   d) hung

8. **If I eat all of these vegetables, mother will let me watch television.**
   a) I and me
   b) mother
   c) television
   d) vegetables

9. **We played with the puppy then fed it a biscuit.**
   a) played
   b) We and it
   c) biscuit
   d) puppy

10. **Have you seen the painting we made?**
    a) have
    b) painting
    c) made
    d) you and we

EXERCISE 2

Tick (✓) the correct pronouns.

1. Me/I am going to the park. My sister is coming with I/me.

2. My mother saw two girls. They/She were at the swing.

3. Us/We saw a gorilla. Did you see them/it?

4. Today is Andrew's birthday. I bought a gift for him/his.

5. I/me want a teacher this/who can guide him/me learn English.

Verbs

Words that denote action are called verbs. They tell us how people, animals or things act.

Sohan **goes** to office in the afternoon. **(What does Sohan do?)**

He **plays** football in the morning. **(What does he do?)**

The words **goes** and **plays** denote action. They are verbs.

There are two kinds of verbs.

Main verb – which has its own meaning (gives, plays, pulls, jumps).

Helping verb – which helps the main verb to change (is, am are, was, were, do, does)

EXERCISE 1

Fill in the blanks with suitable verbs.

1. I _____ books with my pocket money last week.
   a) bought
   b) opened
   c) fly
   d) send

2. The guard _____ the door slowly.
   a) got
   b) opened
   c) threw
   d) caught

3. I _____ the bus because I was late.
   a) ate
   b) rushed
   c) jumped
   d) missed

4. The man _____ from the second floor.
   a) shouted
   b) flew
   c) whispered
   d) launched

5. The students _____ for their team.
   a) knocked
   b) ran
   c) cheered
   d) failed

6. The mice _____ across the kitchen floor.
   a) swam
   b) ran
   c) flew
   d) shouted

7. The man at the counter _____ the money.
   a) drank
   b) threw
   c) counted
   d) pushed

8. Our class _____ the championship.
   a) saw
   b) danced
   c) ran
   d) won

9. My sister likes to _____ on Sundays.
   a) dance
   b) rest
   c) eat
   d) cry

10. My friend _____ to Australia last year.
    a) liked
    b) drowned
    c) went
    d) cook

EXERCISE 2

Choose the correct verbs.

1. **The doctor treats patients with proper care.**
   a) doctor b) patients
   c) proper d) treats

2. **A farmer works in field to grow crops.**
   a) farmer b) grow
   c) works d) crops

3. **Rohan's mother teaches in a new school.**
   a) teaches b) mother
   c) school d) new

4. **That watchman guards our colony at night.**
   a) watchman b) night
   c) that d) guards

5. **My mother cooks delicious food.**
   a) delicious b) mother
   c) cooks d) food

6. **Ashima laughed when she saw the clown.**
   a) clown b) laughed
   c) she d) when

7. **Children of this locality go to the nearby park.**
   a) nearby b) locality
   c) go d) this

8.   Her sister gifted her a toy.
   a) a
   b) gifted
   c) toy
   d) her

9.   Mohan slept early that day.
   a) slept
   b) day
   c) day
   d) early

10.   Sumit ran behind the bus.
   a) ran
   b) behind
   c) bus
   d) not

EXERCISE 3

Circle the suitable verbs in the following sentences.

1.   The trophy (was, were) given to them.
2.   While we (was, were) sleeping, the doorbell rang.
3.   It (was, were) nice to see them having fun.
4.   We (was, were) not able to solve the problem.
5.   We (was, were) proud of ourselves for winning.
6.   It (is, are, am) important that we leave now or we will be late.
7.   I (is, are, am) not busy on Wednesday.
8.   There (was, were) ants everywhere in the old house.
9.   I think option D (is, are) the correct one.
10. Here (is, are, am) your new pack of crayons.

PREPOSITIONS

8

A **preposition** is a word that shows the relation between persons or things.

For example:
The rat is **in** the house.
No, the cat is **outside** the house.
The ball is **under** the table.
Abhishek is writing **in** a notebook.
The pen is kept **on** the board.
Sana is standing **near** the gate.

In the above sentences, coloured words are prepositions.

EXERCISE 1

Read the sentences below and circle the prepositions.

1. Ramesh held the shade over the little girl.
2. The nurse is standing at the door.
3. I fell down the hill and rolled on the grass.
4. The cat sat under the big tree.
5. The children played around the benches.
6. The boy sat on the chair.
7. Our pet dog, Tim, follows my father when he goes for a walk.
8. Nancy searched everywhere and found her pen beside the dressing table.
9. Sam climbed onto the bus.
10. John did not have lunch with us.

EXERCISE 2

Fill in the blanks with suitable prepositions.

1. It was nice _____ meet you.
   a) and b) if
   c) to d) but

2. Don't be late _____ the school.
   a) by b) for
   c) with d) when

3. She is the new teacher _____ Bangalore.
   a) from b) to
   c) by d) but

4. Do you work _____ this place?
   a) out b) in
   c) under d) without

5. Jessica is _____ a holiday.
   a) on b) in
   c) under d) by

6. What is this called _____ your country?
   a) in b) above
   c) near d) over

7. Look _____ the beautiful sunset.
   a) at b) by
   c) in d) above

8. Nayan's birthday is _____ September.
   a) in   b) below
   c) near   d) inside

9. Don't run _____ the road.
   a) inside   b) across
   c) to   d) into

10. Put the box _____ the cupboard.
    a) under   b) next to
    c) through   d) underneath

EXERCISE 3

Fill in the blanks with the correct options:

1. This dish is different _____ that. (from/to/with)
2. You should be nice _____ them. (to/at/with)
3. He has been waiting _____ many days. (since/for/from)
4. I haven't been to my hometown _____ a long time. (since/for/from)
5. He goes _____ the temple every evening. (to/at/on)
6. This is a comfortable house to live _____. (on/at/in)
7. They were called _____ the principal. (by/with/for)
8. We should not spend money _____ such things. (for/on/with)
9. I gave him a chair to sit _____ . (on/at/in)
10. The new show begins _____ Monday. (on/in/from)

CONJUNCTIONS

A word that joins two words, a group of words or sentences is called a **conjunction**.

For example:

I want food **and** water.

Avinash wanted to play **but** it was raining heavily.

Nikita has left early **because** she had fever.

This book **either** belongs to him **or** Rajeev.

And, but, so, because and **or** are some common conjunctions.

EXERCISE 1

Fill in the blanks using suitable conjunctions.

1. **This is a small _____ beautiful city.**
   a) for　　　　　　　　　　　　　　b) or
   c) so　　　　　　　　　　　　　　d) but

2. **Mayank _____ Anu help their mother.**
   a) for　　　　　　　　　　　　　　b) and
   c) after　　　　　　　　　　　　　d) but

3. **I lived in Kolkata _____ I was a child.**
   a) now　　　　　　　　　　　　　b) since
   c) before　　　　　　　　　　　　d) when

4. He ran fast _____ he was late.

a) if b) as

c) though d) because

5. We will visit our uncle _____ grandmother during the summer.

a) but b) to

c) and d) yet

6. Let us wait here _____ he arrives.

a) till b) though

c) than d) that

7. She didn't work hard _____ failed.

a) and b) but

c) yet d) nor

8. I regard Santosh _____ my best student.

a) if b) as

c) after d) that

9. _____ I was suffering from fever I missed the wedding.

a) As b) But

c) If d) Though

10. My sister is busy _____ she is going to China.

a) yet b) and

c) because d) when

EXERCISE 2

Choose the most suitable conjunctions that can be used to join the sentences.

1. **He is going to the club. You cannot go with him.**
   a) and   b) but
   c) as   d) though

2. **She will buy new books. She needs them.**
   a) and   b) because
   c) after   d) though

3. **The child was laughing. He was enjoying the games.**
   a) but   b) yet
   c) nor   d) because

4. **The parcel has arrived. You cannot collect it today.**
   a) and   b) so
   c) yet   d) but

5. **Do you like the dinner? Do you like the snacks?**
   a) and   b) if
   c) or   d) but

Articles

10

An **article** is a word, which is used to modify a noun, i. e., a person, place, object, or idea.

Now read the sentences given below carefully.

There is **a** shop near my house.
I have **an** ice cream from there on every Sunday evening.
This time I will have the chocolate one with **the** blue wrapper.
Did you notice that we use **a** or **an** with singular nouns?
Why do you think we use **the** with the **word chocolate** and **blue**?

A is used with singular words that begin with a consonant sound.

For example:
a bag, **a** chair

An is used with singular words that begin with a vowel sound.

For example:
an object, **an** elephant

The is used with a particular person, animal or thing.

For example:
the Eiffel Tower, the mountain

EXERCISE 1

Correct the following sentences.

1. The Paris is a big city.
   _____

2. A giraffe is not the pet animal.
   _____

3. An honesty is a best policy.

   _____

4. The Dickens was a great writer.

   _____

5. Sun rises in east.

   _____

6. I saw her when she was two-year-old.

   _____

7. Who has not seen street dog?

   _____

8. This is best food I have ever had.

   _____

9. Mahatma Gandhi was great leader of India.

   _____

10. The boy played with ball he bought recently.

    _____

EXERCISE 2

Fill in the correct articles in the given passage.

_____ Taj Mahal is _____ beautiful monument built in 1631 by _____ emperor Shah Jahan in memory of

his wife Mumtaz Mahal. It is situated on _____ banks of river Yamuna at Agra. It looks beautiful in _____ moonlight. _____ Taj Mahal is made up of white marble. In front of _____ monument, there is _____ beautiful garden known as _____ Charbagh. Inside _____ monument, there are two tombs. These tombs are of Shah Jahan and his wife Mumtaz Mahal. _____ Taj Mahal is considered as one of _____ Seven Wonders of _____ World. Many tourists come to see this beautiful structure from different parts of _____ world.

EXERCISE 3

Circle the correct article (a/an/the) in each of the following sentences.

1. Shaun wanted to play a/an game.
2. I saw a/an big diamond in the shop.
3. Tanya quickly finished the/an homework.
4. Mother put rice in a/an pressure cooker.
5. There is a box near a/the bed.
6. Steve visited an/the place again last week.
7. Will you watch the recipe of making an/a eclair on TV?
8. Children insisted that the host tell them an/a story.
9. Mr Raymond is a/an Englishman.
10. Let's go for a/an ride.

Jumbled Words

KCRUT – This is a wrong word because it does not make any sense.

TRUCK – This is a correct word as it has a meaning. A truck is a vehicle used for carrying heavy loads.

The letters in **KCRUT** and **TRUCK** are same but they have been **jumbled** because of which **KCRUT** didn't make any sense.

EXERCISE 1

Write the given jumbled words correctly and then match them with the correct picture.

1. PAPEL   _____

2. MOTATO   _____

3. GIAREFF   _____

4. LABET   _____

5. RAWET   _____

6. CKCIH   _____

7. UPRLEP _____

8. KOBOETON _____

9. GLAF _____

10. WBONIAR _____

11. KISTC _____

12. CARNOY _____

13. OLOSHC _____

14. AODR _____

15. YCLECBI _____

EXERCISE 2

Put the letters of the words in order to make meaningful words.

1. **IRACH**
   a) RAICH					b) HAICR
   c) ARICH					d) CHAIR

2. **LCPIEN**
   a) LIPCEN					b) NIPCEL
   c) LEPCIN					d) PENCIL

3. EORSH

a) ORESH b) ORESH

c) HORSE d) ESROH

4. UNEQE

a) EQENU b) QUEEN

c) ENEUQ d) NEEUQ

5. SLSGA

a) GLASS b) ALGSS

c) SLASG d) SSALG

6. OMNAG

a) GONAM b) ONGAM

c) GANOM d) MANGO

7. ELPTA

a) APTEL b) LEPTA

c) PLATE d) ETALP

8. YDRAI

a) YRDAI b) DRAIY

c) DIARY d) RAIDY

9. NTOTCO

a) NOCTOT b) COTTON

c) NOTTOC d) COOTTN

10. YDIAS

a) SAIDY b) DAISY

c) AIDSY d) ISYDA

Jumbled words in sentences

12

I a student am.

Does the above group of words make sense? No, because the words are not in a correct, meaningful order.

I am a student.

We can understand the above group of words because now the jumbled words are in order and make sense.

EXERCISE 1

Arrange the following group of words in correct order to make meaningful sentences.

1. **writing letter am I a my grandfather to.**

   a. My grandfather a to letter am I writing.
   b. Letter am I writing a my grandfather to.
   c. Am I a my grandfather to writing letter.
   d. I am writing a letter to my grandfather.

2. **working he hard time this is.**

   a. He hard working time this is.
   b. Time this is he hard working.
   c. This time he is working hard.
   d. Is time this he working hard.

3. **may Sonia not able be to this week come.**

   a. Sonia may not be able to come this week.
   b. This week come able may not Sonia to be.
   c. come this week not be able may Sonia to.
   d. Come week this to be able not may Sonia.

47

4. **shop the new beautiful is very.**

   a. New shop beautiful is very the.
   b. Very beautiful the is new shop.
   c. The new shop is very beautiful.
   d. Beautiful is very new the shop.

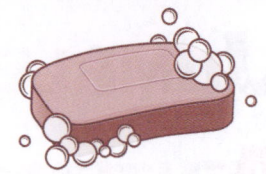

5. **time dinner is it have to.**

   a. It is time to have dinner.
   b. Is dinner time to have it.
   c. Dinner is it have to time.
   d. To have it is dinner time.

6. **go cannot we raining is it because.**

   a. Raining is it because go cannot we.
   b. We raining is it because go cannot.
   c. We cannot go raining is it because.
   d. We cannot go because it is raining.

7. **have I to work finish this tonight by.**

   a. To work finish this tonight by have i.
   b. This tonight by have I to work finish.
   c. I have to finish this work by tonight.
   d. Tonight by work this finish to have i.

8. **must come he tomorrow school to.**

   a. To school tomorrow he must come.
   b. Tomorrow school he come must to.
   c. He must tomorrow school to come.
   d. He must come to school tomorrow.

9. **recently moved has he different city to a.**

   a. Recently moved he has different city a to.
   b. Moved recently he has city different to a.
   c. Moved has recently different city a he to.
   d. He has recently moved to a different city.

10. **the road across market the is.**

    a. Across road the is the market.
    b. The road across the is market.
    c. Is market the road across the.
    d. The market is across the road.

Antonyms and synonyms

Good – Bad   **Near – Far**   **Above – Below**

In the above pair of words, the common thing is that the paired words mean exactly the opposite of each other. Such words are called **antonyms**.

Begin – Start   **Difficult – Hard**   **Disturb – Trouble**

Here, the paired words have same or almost similar meaning to each other. These words are called **synonyms**.

EXERCISE 1

Choose the correct options.

1. **Synonym of wonderful:**
   a) terrible
   b) dreadful
   c) awful
   d) delightful

2. **Antonym of fast:**
   a) slow
   b) swift
   c) quick
   d) rapid

3. **Antonym of clean:**
   a) neat
   b) tidy
   c) dirty
   d) was

4. **Antonym of night:**
   a) noon
   b) day
   c) morning
   d) evening

5. **Synonym of strong:**
   a) powerful
   b) timid
   c) sick
   d) weak

6. **Synonym of small:**
   a) huge
   b) many
   c) tiny
   d) big

7. **Antonym of huge:**
   a) massive
   b) giant
   c) enormous
   d) small

8. **Antonym of quick:**
   a) slow
   b) bore
   c) timid
   d) fast

9. **Antonym of husband:**
   a) mother
   b) sister
   c) daughter
   d) wife

10. **Synonym of faithful:**
    a) loyal
    b) cruel
    c) cheat
    d) cunning

EXERCISE 2

Choose the correct antonyms of the underlined words.

1. **Her house is very ugly.**
   a) unattractive
   b) dirty
   c) weird
   d) beautiful

2. **He saw a lion in the forest.**
    a) under   b) above

    c) in   d) below

3. **Our plane flew below the Pacific Ocean.**
    a) in   b) above

    c) near   d) under

4. **Dirty the room quickly.**
    a) Untidy   b) Messy

    c) Ugly   d) Clean

5. **My wild cat's name is Peet.**
    a) pet   b) feral

    c) untamed   d) fierce

Story Writing

Writing stories helps in improving the usage of words to explain a situation.

Key points to remember:

- A story has a title.
- The language should be simple.
- Events should be described in order.
- The ending should be reasonable.

EXERCISE 1

Write a story with the help of the given keywords.

Morning	Sunday	bright sun	beautiful	mother
newspaper	father	garden	sister	drawing
father	calls suddenly	in the garden	surprise	to the corner
two little chicks	very excited			

_____

_____

_____

_____

_____

_____

EXERCISE 2

Write a short story on the topic Friendship.

_____
_____
_____
_____
_____
_____
_____

EXERCISE 3

Fill in the blanks to complete the story.

_____ a king, _____ monkey. This monkey was a fool _____ _____ the king's palace. He was also allowed to _____ king's _____ rooms _____ _____ not allowed. One afternoon, _____ was asleep, while the monkey _____. _____ a fly came _____ and sat on the king's chest. The monkey shooed her away, but the fly _____ and return on the king's chest again. The monkey got _____ and excited. The foolish monkey started _____ with a sword. The fly _____ king's chest again, _____ hit the fly with all his might. The fly _____ unharmed, _____ severely wounded.

53

ANALOGY

Analogy is a comparison between two things that are related to each other in some way for the purpose of explaining a situation.

For example:
Tea: cup
Pen: paper
Needle: thread

EXERCISE 1

Choose the correct analogies in the following:

1. **Grocer**
   a) shop b) car
   c) cycle d) home

2. **Sailor**
   a) plane b) bus
   c) truck d) ship

3. **Petrol**
   a) car b) cycle
   c) shoes d) water

4. **Bread**
   a) bun b) cake
   c) pudding d) butter

5. **Lock**
   a) door
   b) window
   c) latch
   d) key

EXERCISE 2

Choose suitable words from the given options and fill in the blanks.

1. **Lawyer is to court; cashier is to_____.**
   a) park
   b) school
   c) garden
   d) bank

2. **Artist is to paint; photographer is to _____.**
   a) camera
   b) bus
   c) pen
   d) car

3. **Car is to garage; stove is to_____.**
   a) bedroom
   b) bathroom
   c) kitchen
   d) terrace

4. **Table is to furniture; shirt is to _____.**
   a) footwear
   b) clothing
   c) food
   d) vehicle

5. **Tired is to sleep; hungry is to_____.**
   a) food
   b) water
   c) rain
   d) anger

Model Test Paper-I

Read the given passage and answer the questions.

Once upon a time, there was an old woman who lived in a small cottage. One day, she decided to make something special for her husband. She made dough and rolled it flat. She put cherries to make buttons and raisins to make two eyes and a mouth. She cut the dough in the shape of a gingerbread man. She put the gingerbread man in the oven to bake. Soon she heard a voice from the oven, "Let me out! Let me out!" When the old woman opened the oven door, she was surprised to see the gingerbread man jump and run out of the cottage shouting, "Don't eat me." The old woman ran after the gingerbread man. "Stop! Stop!" she said. But the gingerbread man ran on saying, "Run, run as fast as you can. You can't catch me, I'm the gingerbread man".

1. The old woman cut the dough in the shape of a _____.
    a) gingerbread man b) garlic man
    c) cookie uncle d) pan pizza

2. "Run, run as fast as you can. You can't _____ me, I'm the gingerbread man."
    a) pull b) catch
    c) push d) hit

3. The woman decided to make something for her_____.
    a) brother b) husband
    c) son d) daughter

4. She lived in a_____.
    a) cottage b) hut
    c) tent d) house

Fill in the blanks with correct verbs.

5. I_____ five hundred rupees. (has/have/had)

6. Ananya _____ a new bicycle. (has/have/had)
7. The children _____ in the lawn. (runs/run)

Write the correct nouns.

8. There were many _____ in the hospital.
   a) patients   b) players
   c) postmen   d) soldiers

9. The _____ caught the robbers.
   a) cobbler   b) doctor
   c) policeman   d) florist.

10. _____ should respect their elders.
    a) Children   b) Boys
    c) Girls   d) Animals

Tick (✓) D for declarative, I for interrogative, E for exclamatory and IM for imperative sentences.

11. The movie was so nice!
    D   I   E   IM

12. When will you come back from Mumbai?
    D   I   E   IM

13. The books are on the table.
    D   I   E   IM

Choose the correct prepositions.

14. The book is _____ Rima
    a) in   b) on
    c) under   d) for

15. Let's go _____ the park.
    a) to
    b) above
    c) under
    d) for

16. The taxi is _____ the gate
    a) on
    b) in
    c) over
    d) at

Choose the correct conjunctions and fill in the blanks.

17. This is his car _____ his house.
    a) and
    b) but
    c) since
    d) or

18. Wait here _____ I come back.
    a) but
    b) and
    c) or
    d) till

19. He had reached _____ me.
    a) but
    b) and
    c) as
    d) before

20. He will be leaving today _____ tomorrow.
    a) but
    b) or
    c) and
    d) if

Fill in the blanks with correct articles.

21. This is _____ nice car. (a/an/the)

22. _____ show is about to start. (An/The/A)

23. She studies in _____ university. (an/the/a)

24. We will reach there in _____ hour. (a/an/the)

Choose the correct synonyms.

25. Cute
    a) ugly b) angry
    c) big d) lovable

26. Old
    a) unique b) ancient
    c) modern d) new

27. Scared
    a) smart b) afraid
    c) rude d) fast

Choose the correct antonyms.

28. Accept
    a) Begin b) Allow
    c) Brave d) Refuse

29. Danger
    a) Warm b) Bright
    c) Easy d) Safety

30. Clean
    a) Ugly b) Bad
    c) Dirty d) Cheap

MODEL TEST PAPER-2

Read the given passage and answer the questions.

One summer's day, in a field, a Grasshopper was hopping about, playing with toys, chirping and singing. An Ant passed by, carrying along with great toil an ear of corn to its nest. "Come and play with me," said the Grasshopper, "instead of panting and gasping."

"I am collecting food for the winter," said the Ant, "and you should also do so." "Why think of winter?" said the Grasshopper, "we have got lots of food for now." But the Ant went on its way and continued its work. When the winter came, the Grasshopper had no food and was dying of hunger. It saw the ants eating corn from the stores they had collected in past. Then the Grasshopper knew: One should always be prepared for the days ahead.

Tick (✓) Y for Yes and N for No.

1. The Ant and the Grasshopper met in a park.
    Y   N

2. The Grasshopper wanted to collect food for winter.
    Y   N

3. The Grasshopper wanted to help the Ant.
    Y   N

4. The Ant collected food for winter.
    Y   N

Choose the correct pronouns for the underlined words.

5. My father is in the office.
    a) He   b) They
    c) Us   d) She

6. <u>Mom and I</u> went to the market in the evening.
   a) We
   b) Us
   c) Our
   d) They

7. <u>The dog</u> is wagging its tail.
   a) He
   b) She
   c) It
   d) You

Rearrange the jumbled letters to make meaningful words.

8. CHERTEA
   a) TEARHCE
   b) CHRETEA
   c) TEACHER
   d) HETAERC

9. TAWRE
   a) WEART
   b) TREAW
   c) REAWT
   d) WATER

10. REMMUS
    a) MERMUS
    b) SUMREM
    c) SUMMER
    d) MERSUM

11. SCOLOH
    a) OCSLOH
    b) HOLSCO
    c) HOLOCS
    d) SCHOOL

Arrange the group of words in order to make meaningful sentences.

12. Stella met park in the me.
    a. Park in the me met Stella.
    b. Met me the Stella park in.
    c. Stella park me in the met.
    d. Stella met me in the park.

13. cows of herd has a uncle.
    a. Herd of cows has a uncle
    b. Uncle a has cows of herd
    c. Uncle has a herd of cows.
    d. Herd of uncle has a cows.

14. team win will this game our.
    a. Will our game win this team.
    b. Game our will team this win.
    c. Win this team will our game.
    d. Our team will win this game.

Write the correct analogy.

15. Lion
    a) zoo
    b) shed
    c) group
    d) den

16. Horse
    a) man
    b) animal
    c) shoe
    d) stable

17. Fish
    a) pond
    b) den
    c) nest
    d) kennel

Choose the correct antonyms of the following words.

18. Care
    a) Pamper
    b) Love
    c) Like
    d) Neglect

19. Defeat
    a) Victory
    b) Good
    c) Learn
    d) Loose

20. War
    a) Anarchy
    b) Anger
    c) Peace
    d) Lack

21. Answer
    a) Say   b) Respond
    c) Reply   d) Question

22. Cool
    a) Warm   b) Normal
    c) Freeze   d) Cool

Choose the correct synonyms.

23. Allow
    a) Stop   b) Restrict
    c) Permit   d) Hurdle

24. Danger
    a) Colourful   b) Pale
    c) Smooth   d) Threat

25. Smooth
    a) Hollow   b) Under
    c) Beneath   d) Uniform

26. Good
    a) Weird   b) Rough
    c) Bad   d) Nice

27. Slow
    a) Pace   b) Speed
    c) Quick   d) Sluggish

Choose the correct articles to fill in the blanks.

28. I need ____ appointment with the doctor. (a/an/the)

29. _____ plane is about to take off. (The/An/A)

30. _____ glass of water will be good. (An/A/The)

MODEL TEST PAPER-3

Read the given passage and answer the questions.

A place where different animals and birds are kept is called a zoo. Zoo attracts children a lot. Last Sunday I went to see the zoo. We bought the tickets and went inside. Many people were already there to see the animals and birds. We saw the lion first. Then we saw some tigers. After that we went to the enclosures of leopards, elephants, bears and foxes. We also went to see the monkeys and birds. The monkeys were jumping from one branch of the tree to another. Some monkeys were eating bananas. The birds in the zoo were very beautiful. I saw some birds for the first time. Then we moved to a tank. It was full of crocodiles. We also saw some other water birds like ducks and cranes. We then saw snakes such as pythons and cobras. We spent six hours in the zoo and then came back. We enjoyed a lot there.

1. Who are more attracted to the zoo?
    a) children
    b) boys
    c) girls
    d) adults

2. What do monkeys like to eat?
    a) apples
    b) oranges
    c) grapes
    d) bananas

3. Where do monkeys live?
    a) den
    b) cave
    c) water
    d) trees

4. In a zoo, leopards are kept in:
    a) cages
    b) enclosures
    c) caves
    d) dens

5. Crocodiles like to live in:
   a) water
   b) holes
   c) burrows
   d) trees

Choose the correct verbs and fill in the blanks.

6. We should _____ lots of water.
   a) drink
   b) eat
   c) throw
   d) float

7. Let's ____ to the end of the road.
   a) dance
   b) crawl
   c) run
   d) fall

8. Bamboo trees _____ very fast.
   a) fall
   b) move
   c) shake
   d) grow

Choose the correct nouns.

9. Russia is the largest _____ in the world.
   a) country
   b) city
   c) lake
   d) river

10. Sally found a _____ of coins in the store room.
    a) bunch
    b) group
    c) bundle
    d) collection

11. A new _____ came to the school.
    a) teacher
    b) notebook
    c) uniform
    d) book

12. Do you see those ducks swimming in the _____?
    a) tub
    b) bucket
    c) bathtub
    d) pond

Tick (✓) D for declarative, I for interrogative, E for exclamatory and IM for imperative sentences.

13. Do you want a mango ice cream?
    D   I   E   IM

14. She wants to buy a bunch of flowers.
    D   I   E   IM

15. The sunset is so beautiful!
    D   I   E   IM

16. She is sitting on a big rocking chair.
    D   I   E   IM

17. I love to draw an aeroplane.
    D   I   E   IM

18. A horse likes to eat grass.
    D   I   E   IM

Choose the correct prepositions to fill in the blanks.

19. The toy is _____ the shelf.
    a) of   b) to
    c) on   d) for

20. I will see you _____ lunch time.
    a) along   b) of
    c) on   d) at

21. The girl _____ the yellow dress will sing.
    a) on   b) under
    c) near   d) in

22. The children are sitting _____ the classroom.
    a) above b) below
    c) in   d) down

Fill in the blanks with correct articles.

23. I will change _____ bedsheet before sleeping. (a/an/the)

24. Is _____ blue shirt yours? (a/an/the)

25. The train is running late by _____ hour. (a/an/the)

26. You must meet _____ expert. (a/an/the)

27. You were knocking at _____ door very hard. (a/an/the)

Choose the correct conjunctions to fill in the blanks.

28. Rahul _____ Rajiv are brothers.
    a) and   b) but
    c) since d) or

29. Nayan wanted to come _____ it was very hot.
    a) and   b) if
    c) but   d) as

30. Children love to eat cakes _____ chocolates.
    a) because b) so
    c) or   d) and

ANSWER KEY

Chapter 1

Exercise 1
1. d   2. d   3. d   4. a   5. b

Exercise 2
1. b   2. d   3. c   4. c   5. d

Exercise 3
1. c   2. d   3. c   4. d   5. d

Exercise 4
Students to attempt on their own. Answers may vary.

Exercise 5
1. c   2. d   3. d   4. c

Exercise 6
1. a   2. a   3. b   4. d   5. d

Exercise 7
1. d   2. c   3. c   4. d   5. a

Exercise 8
1. a   2. b   3. b   4. b

Chapter 2

Exercise 1
1. YES   2. NO   3. NO   4. YES   5. NO
6. YES   7. NO   8. YES   9. YES   10. NO

Exercise 2
Students to attempt on their own. Answers may vary.

Exercise 3
Peter and Nancy are brother and sister. Peter is nine and Nancy is eleven years old. They live in the city near a school. They play after school. They also help their mother in the evening.

Exercise 4
1. I   2. D   3. E   4. IM   5. E
6. I   7. D   8. IM   9. I   10. D

Chapter 3

Exercise 1
Students to attempt on their own. Answers may vary.

Exercise 2
Students to attempt on their own. Answers may vary.

Exercise 3
1. a 2. c 3. a 4. d 5. a

Chapter 4

Exercise 1
Students to attempt on their own. Answers may vary.

Exercise 2
Common Nouns: city, month, man, game, country, dog
Proper Nouns: Sunday, Christmas, Rima, Red fort, Mickey Mouse, Mars

Exercise 3
1. woman   flower   book
2. school   city   cat
3. chips
4. England   house   boy
5. music   fire

Exercise 4
Proper Nouns
1. India 2. October 3. Audi 4. Bible 5. Sydney
6. Diwali 7. Amazon 8. Asia 9. Earth 10. Sam
11. Christmas 12. Batman 13. New Delhi 14. Google 15. Naina

Chapter 5

Exercise 1
1. a 2. b 3. a 4. a 5. b
6. c 7. a 8. a 9. b 10. b

Exercise 2
happiness   sadness   kindness   strength   bravery
excitement   hope   confidence   sorrow

Exercise 3
1. a 2. d 3. d 4. a 5. d
6. a 7. a 8. d 9. b 10. a

Exercise 4
1. a 2. a 3. a 4. c 5. a
6. b 7. a 8. a 9. b 10. a

Chapter 6

Exercise 1
1. a 2. c 3. d 4. c 5. d
6. b 7. a 8. a 9. b 10. d

Exercise 2
    1. I, me   2. They   3. We, it   4. him   5. I, who, me

Chapter 7
Exercise 1
    1. a   2. b   3. d   4. a   5. c
    6. b   7. c   8. d   9. a   10. c

Exercise 2
    1. d   2. c   3. a   4. d   5. c
    6. b   7. c   8. b   9. a   10. a

Exercise 3
    1. was   2. were   3. was   4. were   5. were
    6. is   7. am   8. were   9. is   10. is

Chapter 8
Exercise 1
    1. over   2. at   3. down, on   4. under   5. around
    6. on   7. for   8. beside   9. onto   10. with

Exercise 2
    1. c   2. b   3. a   4. b   5. a
    6. a   7. a   8. a   9. b   10. b

Exercise 3
    1. from   2. to   3. for   4. for   5. to
    6. in   7. by   8. on   9. on   10. on

Chapter 9
Exercise 1
    1. d   2. b   3. d   4. d   5. c
    6. a   7. a   8. as   9. a   10. c

Exercise 2
    1. b   2. b   3. b   4. d   5. c

Chapter 10

Exercise 1
1. Paris is a big city.
2. Giraffe is not a pet animal.
3. Honesty is the best policy.
4. Dickens was a great writer.
5. The Sun rises in the east.
6. I saw her when she was a two-year-old.
7. Who has not seen a street dog?
8. This is the best food I have ever had.

9. Mahatma Gandhi was a great leader of India.
10. The boy played with the ball he bought recently.

Exercise 2
The, a, the, the, the, The, the, a, the, the, The, the, the, the

Exercise 3
1. a	2. a	3. the	4. a	5. the
6. the	7. an	8. a	9. an	10. a

Chapter 11
Exercise 1
1. APPLE	2. TOMATO	3. GIRAFFE	4. TABLE	5. WATER
6. CHICK	7. PURPLE	8. NOTEBOOK	9. FLAG	10. RAINBOW
11. STICK	12. CRAYON	13. SCHOOL	14. ROAD	15. BICYCLE

Exercise 2
1. d	2. d	3. c	4. b	5. a
6. d	7. c	8. c	9. b	10. b

Chapter 12
Exercise 1
1. d	2. c	3. a	4. c	5. a
6. d	7. c	8. d	9. d	10. d

Chapter 13
Exercise 1
1. d	2. a	3. c	4. b	5. a
6. c	7. d	8. a	9. d	10. a

Exercise 2
1. d	2. c	3. b	4. d	5. a

Chapter 14
Exercise 1
Students to attempt on their own. Answers may vary.

Exercise 2
Students to attempt on their own. Answers may vary.

Exercise 3
Once there was a king, who had a pet monkey. This monkey was a fool, but was treated royally and moved freely in the king's palace. He was also allowed to enter the king's personal rooms where even the servants were not allowed. One afternoon, the king was asleep, while the monkey kept a watch. All of a sudden, a fly came in the room and sat on the king's chest. The monkey swayed her away, but the fly would only go away for some time and return on the king's chest again.

The monkey got very angry and excited. The foolish monkey started chasing the fly with a sword. The fly sat on the king's chest again, the monkey hit the fly with all his might. The fly flew away unharmed, but the king was severely wounded.

Chapter 15

Exercise 1

1. a   2. d   3. a   4. d   5. d

Exercise 2

1. d   2. a   3. c   4. b   5. a

Model Test Paper-1

1. a 2. b 3. b 4. a 5. have 6. has 7. run 8. a 9. c 10. a 11. E 12. I 13. D 14. d 15. a 16. d 17. a 18. d 19. d 20. b 21. a 22. The 23. a 24. an 25. d 26. b 27. b 28. d 29. d 30. c

Model Test Paper-2

1. N 2. N 3. N 4. Y 5. a 6. a 7. c 8. c 9. d 10. c 11. d 12. d 13. c 14. d 15. d 16. d 17. a 18. d 19. a 20. c 21. d 22. a 23. c 24. d 25. d 26. d 27. d 28. an 29. The 30. A

Model Test Paper-3

1. a 2. d 3. d 4. b 5. a 6. a 7. c 8. d 9. a 10. d 11. a 12. d 13. I 14. D 15. E 16. D 17. D 18. D 19. c 20. d 21. d 22. c 23. the 24. the 25. an 26. an 27. the 28. a 29. c 30. d